THEN AND THERE SERIES

GENERAL EDITOR

MARJORIE REEVES, M.A., Ph.D.

London in the Eighteenth Century

JULIET DYMOKE

Illustrated from contemporary sources by

G. FRY

D1340807

LONGMAN

LONGMAN GROUP LIMITED
London

*Associated companies, branches and representatives
throughout the world*

First published 1958
Tenth impression 1979

ISBN 0 582 20369 4

Acknowledgments

For permission to include drawings based on copyright material we
are indebted to the following: Guildhall Library–pages 3 and 73 (foot);
Trustees of the Tate Gallery–pages 7 and 55; Guildhall Museum–
page 16; Faber & Faber–pages 19-22 from *Allen: The Story of Clothes;*
Victoria & Albert Museum, Crown Copyright–pages 26, 47 and 65;
National Portrait Gallery–page 39; Lord Harmsworth–page 40; Country
Life–page 45 (foot); Bodleian Library–page 54; Macmillan & Co Ltd–
page 79 from *Green: A Short History of the English People, Vol. IV.*

*Printed in Hong Kong by
The Hong Kong Printing Press (1977) Ltd*

CONTENTS

	Page
LONDON TWO HUNDRED YEARS AGO	1
A WALK ROUND THE TOWN	6
FANNY BURNEY AND HER FAMILY	18
Their Clothes	19
Their Home	23
Food and Drink	27
Daily Lessons and Schools	29
Going to Church	32
FAMOUS VISITORS IN ST. MARTIN'S STREET	35
HOW THE RICH PEOPLE ENJOYED THEMSELVES	42
Theatres and Pleasure Gardens	47
Coffee Houses and Clubs	53
LIFE IN THE HOUSE OF ROBERT GIBBON, DRAPER	58
What it was like to be an apprentice	67
WHEN YOU WERE ILL	71
THE LORD MAYOR AND THE CITY OF LONDON	75
London in a Panic	78
HIS MAJESTY THE KING	81
GOODBYE LONDON	84
HOW WE CAN FIND 'THEN' IN LONDON NOW	85
THINGS TO MAKE AND DO	88
GLOSSARY	91

TO THE READER

Every fact in this book comes from some record written at the time the book is describing; nothing has been invented in these pages, which seek to be a true record of the life and thought of the people who lived in London during the middle years of the eighteenth century. The diaries and letters and books they wrote are original sources to which historians have to go back for their information.

In the same way, every picture in this book is based on a drawing made by someone who lived then and there.

By studying what people said in word and picture about themselves, you will come to feel at home in one 'patch' of the history of the past and really live with the group of people as they thought and worked then and there. And gradually you will be able to fill in more patches of history.

As you read, you will sometimes find a word written like *this*. You can find the meaning of these words in the Glossary on page 91. If there are other words you do not know, look for their meanings in your dictionary.

LONDON TWO HUNDRED YEARS AGO

LISTEN to the noises of London as you wake up tomorrow morning. Most of them are the same as in any other town today—the noise of motor-cars and lorries and buses, the sound of an express train off on its journey to another town or of an aeroplane on its way to another country or continent. Near the river you may hear a ship's siren hooting, and in some places you can hear the low rumble of an underground train.

Now listen to London two hundred years ago. The sounds are very different. Can you hear the rumble of cart-wheels and the clatter of horses' hooves as the big carts roll into the city from the country, laden with fresh fruit and vegetables for the markets? These heavy carts make a great deal of noise on the cobblestones, and the drivers are calling to their horses or shouting to other drivers who get in their way in the narrow streets.

Can you hear the street-cries? Many people sell their goods in the streets and they all have their own special cries—the apple-woman, the bellows-mender, the milk-girl, and many others sell every kind of article from matches, doormats, brooms, baskets, and lavender to hot ginger-bread, muffins, rabbits, and each of the fruits in its proper season.

I

In the pictures below you can see a girl selling baskets, and a man selling old clothes. How does the girl carry her baskets? Do you notice that the man has several hats for sale balanced on top of his own hat?

Other street-cries you might hear are:
"Buy my duke cherries. Quite ripe, sir."
"Buy my fresh mackerel."
"A bed mat or a door mat."

In those days London was much smaller than it is now, so the street sellers did not have to walk as far to sell their goods as they would today.

London today covers an area of over 700 square miles and is the largest city in the world, but if you look at the map on page 4 you will see that it was really quite a small place two hundred years ago. In those days there was no building north of Portland Street where the B.B.C. now stands, or beyond Tottenham Court Road and, further to the east, Old Street. Islington and Hampstead were villages then, across the fields to the north of the City.

To the east the buildings thinned out near the docks—a very busy part of London these days—and Mile End was still a small market town. To the west many wealthy people lived in fine houses round Grosvenor Square and near St. James's Palace and Hyde Park, but Kensington and Chelsea were no more than little villages and a good many of the rich folk built their country houses in the pleasant countryside beyond. South of the Thames there was very little building beyond Kennington Common; the fields and orchards were only a short walk down the Kent Road.

You probably know that London was a walled city once, but in the eighteenth century no one bothered much about the walls, though the gates round the City remained in use. Here are pictures of two of them. Temple Bar was at the western boundary of 'the City', but London had spread well beyond this in 1750.

Newgate

Temple Bar

3

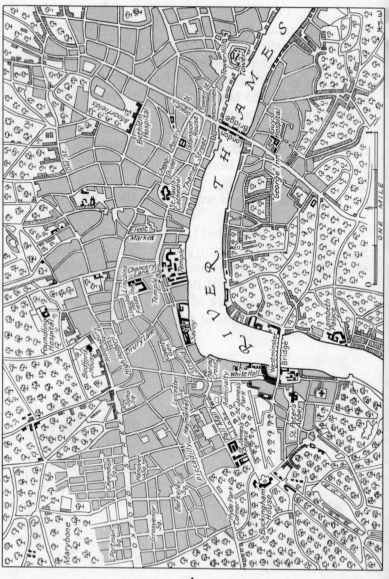

4

How do we know the size and shape of London two hundred years ago? Old drawings and maps are our chief source of knowledge. There are a good many old prints—black-and-white drawings—to be seen: you can often find them in the windows of second-hand bookshops. The map opposite was made by John Roque in 1746. He was a very good *topographer*—a grand name for a map-maker—and his maps are very accurate. If you look at the picture below you will see how he measured the roads when he was making his map. This picture is of Hyde Park Corner. Do you see in the right-hand corner a man with a wheel at the end of two handles? The wheel measures 8 feet 3 inches round the circumference, that is all round the edge, and as the man walks along the machine records how many times the wheel turns. So he has only to multiply that by the circumference to see how far he has gone.

Now we will take a walk round London two hundred years ago.

A WALK ROUND THE TOWN

We get down from the coach or waggon in which we have travelled up from the country to find ourselves, one morning in 1760, in the busy courtyard of the George Inn at Southwark. Coaches drive in and out under the archway, horses and riders come and go, and there is bustle everywhere. The grooms and *ostlers* see to the horses and baggage, and coachmen call to their passengers to make ready while the landlord and his servants hurry to and fro to see that their guests are comfortable.

Here is a fine picture of the George Inn:

From this inn and others like it, people set out on their journeys from London to the south, or they arrived here from as far off as the West Country. Many inns had the picturesque *galleries* you can see, some of them decorated with plants and creepers. Strolling players performed their plays in the courtyard while the audience sat in the galleries. These inns were like our railway stations, for everyone travelled by coach or rode on horseback and the

6

inns provided suitable starting-places and rest-houses on the way for the stage-coaches which carried people to and from London.

When we leave the courtyard of the George Inn, we are on our way to the City, over London Bridge. You will be surprised as you step on to the bridge, for it is not just a simple road across the River Thames, as our bridges are today. It looks more like a street. Coaches and carts, and people walking on either side without any pavement, make the bridge very crowded. There are houses built on each side of the bridge and the road between them is barely twenty feet wide. But the houses are in very bad repair and big arches of strong timber have some-times been built from the top of one house right across the road to the top of the one opposite, to keep them up. In fact an Act of Parliament has just been passed, providing for the removal of these tumble-down houses on the bridge. This is how the houses looked on the bridge:

If we stand where one of the houses has already been pulled down, we can watch the boats on the river. The many arches hold up the current of the river so much that it is a skilled business to 'shoot' the arches to the lower level of the water below. Many people travel by water. Rich men own barges, and there are hundreds of *watermen*, who earn their living by ferrying people up and down the river for a shilling or two, and delivering all sorts of goods.

We could stand here all day and watch the people and the traffic, but there is so much to see that we had better go on. We will walk up Gracechurch Street and then down Thames Street. Here there are busy merchants hurrying along, shopkeepers showing their wares, and all the street-traders whose cries we are beginning to know by now. This is what we see in Gracechurch Street:

Can you see the shop signs hanging over the doors to tell us what kind of a shop each one is? And can you see the man driving his sheep and cows to market? Perhaps he's going to Leadenhall market, which is still a market today, though there is far too much traffic to take animals to market this way in London now.

Can you see the posts along the road by the side of the shops? There is no pavement, so these posts safeguard walkers from the danger of being knocked down by carriages. You can also tie the reins of your horse to one of these posts to make sure your horse does not wander away while you go into a house or shop.

As we go along you will notice that the streets are very dusty and dirty compared with the streets of today. There is mud and rubbish everywhere, for there are no dustbins to be regularly emptied: people just throw everything into the street. Be careful you don't slip on an old cabbage leaf or a piece of fish skin! There is a narrow trench called a *kennel* running down the centre of most streets. This is supposed to carry away the rain-water, but it is always choked with mud and rubbish, so you can imagine how smelly the streets become in hot weather.

There are crowds of people here in the City going about their daily business—but there are many beggars too, for there are a great many very poor people in London, and the parish does not give them much help. Two hundred years ago a man who was out of work or ill would starve unless some charity gave him food, and widows and orphans often had a very hard life. There are some very bad slums in this old London too, and some districts where no respectable person dares to set foot after dark. Though there are lanterns in the streets at night, we should think their light dim compared with present-day street-lighting.

Have you noticed the people who seem to be reciting verses and who try to get you to buy one of the papers they are waving in their hands? These are the *Ballad*-mongers. Whenever something particular happens in London, such as the execution of a well-known highway-man or the arrival of an important person from abroad, the ballad-mongers quickly print a ballad about it and sell it in the street.

Now we have reached London's wonderful cathedral. See how the dome rises above the houses of London:

Old St. Paul's was burned down during the Great Fire of 1666, and this fine new building was built on its ruins by Sir Christopher Wren. It is still new to the Londoners of two hundred years ago, for the last stone of the great building was laid only forty years before in 1710. Its magnificent dome rides high above the City with the golden cross sparkling in the sunlight.

St. Paul's is the Londoner's chief place of worship, used for all special services, royal occasions, and national thanksgivings, and there is a fine choir. Many people visit the cathedral to hear the music of Purcell, Byrd or Handel. You will learn more about Handel later on in this book. However, a good many people go to St. Paul's not to worship or listen to the music, but simply to gossip and meet their friends. For the nave of the great cathedral—that is, the wide centre part stretching from the west door to the portion beneath the circular dome—is used as a meeting-place and a promenade.

This picture shows you what the nave of St. Paul's looked like:

There are no chairs in the nave and you can see the people walking up and down. We should think it rather irreverent these days to use a church as a place to meet and exchange news with your friends, but in the eighteenth century nobody thought it at all odd. Londoners have always been very proud of their beautiful cathedral; and from the gallery outside the dome you get a magnificent view of London. Inside the dome there is the famous Whispering Gallery. If you stand on one side and whisper a message to the wall, your friend on the opposite side—a distance of 107 feet—can hear every word quite clearly. If you can visit St. Paul's you must not forget to climb up to the Whispering Gallery.

From St. Paul's Cathedral we walk down Ludgate Hill and at the bottom cross the Fleet bridge over the Fleet Ditch, a stream that runs into the Thames (but which in twentieth-century London has long since disappeared from sight into a *sewer*). This brings us into Fleet Street, leaving behind us on the right the gloomy Fleet Prison for people who cannot pay their debts. We walk under Temple Bar, where the City ends, and into the Strand. Here there are some very fine houses. In the picture below we have just walked under the archway of Temple Bar.

A good many wealthy people have built their houses in the Strand and the area round about. But the Savoy Palace, a great house in the thirteenth century, is, in 1760, little more than a ruin, though some parts are still good enough to be used as offices for the King's printing press, a prison for deserters, and churches for various foreigners —French, Dutch and Germans. Today only the Savoy Chapel remains; the Savoy Hotel stands now where part of the Savoy Palace used to be.

Here is Northumberland House, built by the Duke of Northumberland:

Can you see the statue of King Charles I? That statue can still be seen today at Charing Cross facing down Whitehall; many people think it is one of the finest statues in London. Northumberland House is not there any more, but today, in the gardens on the left of Villiers Street by Charing Cross station, you can still see an old arched gateway which is all that is left of another great house close by. This was the water-gate of York House, where visitors could land from boats on the river. All along the Strand there used to be these large fashionable houses, backing on to the river, but by the time of our walk many have been pulled down or are in a bad state of repair, for fashionable London is now living further west, round the new Squares.

Now let us go down Whitehall. The King's Palace occupies both sides of the street here, and in the picture below you can see the great *Banqueting* Hall on the left— it is still there today:

This is a very interesting picture as there is so much to notice in it. See how many things of interest you can pick out before you read on.

Now—I wonder if you have seen as much as I have. First there is a group of soldiers on parade on the left.

Then in the centre at the bottom are two men carrying a box-like object. This is called a *sedan-chair*, and just behind the soldiers you can see a sedan-chair rank (just like our taxi ranks).

Did you notice the three coaches? These probably belong to noble folk who have been to the Palace to see the King. And on the right is a Clock Tower: it has just been built—two hundred years ago—and today it still stands above the entrance where the Horse Guards in scarlet and black mount guard on their horses each side of the gates. Today you can walk through the archway under the Clock Tower to the Horse Guards Parade, where many famous ceremonies are held—such as the Trooping of the Colour on the Queen's Birthday.

Beyond the Parade lies St. James's Park, with a lake and trees, and beds full of flowers in summer. When Charles II was King he was particularly fond of this park. He planted many of the trees under whose shade we now walk, and he brought ducks and cranes and other waterfowl to live and breed on a little island in the lake. There are still ducks on the island, though two hundred years ago they called the lake 'the canal', and this tells us that then its sides were straight; the eighteenth century liked straight lines and stiff patterns in its parks much more than we do today. Two names still tell of the things we would have seen two hundred years ago—Birdcage Walk and *Cockpit* Stairs.

Like King Charles, eighteenth-century Londoners enjoy walking in St. James's Park, and they meet here in summer for refreshments in the tea-gardens. In fact, everywhere we go in the London two hundred years ago we find coffee-houses, tea-gardens and *taverns*, for these are the places where people meet and a good deal of business is done in them. Each tavern has its painted sign hanging outside and they make the London streets look very gay. Here are two of them:

Now we come to Westminster Abbey. It looks today just as it did two hundred years ago, for the last part of the building, the twin towers at the west end, was completed in 1739. I expect many of you have visited this famous church, which is our national shrine where so many famous Englishmen are buried and where most of our Kings and Queens have been crowned.

Below is a picture of Westminster Bridge and the Abbey; it was drawn in 1747. The bridge had just been built. You can tell from the number of boats on the river how many people used in those days to travel on the water.

Well, we have walked round a good deal of old London, so it is time to go inside some houses and see how people lived at home in those days.

FANNY BURNEY AND HER FAMILY

In 1760—the year that George III came to the throne—
a certain Dr. Burney brought his family of six children
to live in London. He was evidently a very pleasant gentleman for everybody seems to have liked him. He was a
clever musician, and as soon as he was settled in London
he began giving music lessons to the wealthy society
people. He was welcome everywhere, so if we see what
sort of life he and his family enjoyed, we shall get a good
idea of what eighteenth-century London was like for the
richer folk.

Dr. Burney had two boys. Charles was clever and very
kind; James was a much stronger-minded boy. When
James grew up, he sailed round the world with the famous
Captain Cook. But in 1760 nobody knew yet that there
was such a country as Australia, which Captain Cook
discovered.

There were four little girls in the Burney family.
Esther was very musical like her father; Susan was the
clever one; Charlotte was a little fat dumpling of a girl;
and Fanny was sweet-natured, but rather shy and retiring.
Her parents did not guess that one day Fanny would
be a famous writer, and that from her story EVELINA
we should learn a great deal about the world of fashion in
her day. See if you can find a copy of this book in your
library and read how Evelina came to London two
hundred years ago.

18

Their clothes

Would you like to know what sort of clothes Fanny and her family would be wearing?

Here is a picture of a boy and a girl. I should think the little girl found her skirts getting in the way when she played ball with her brother!

You can see from this picture the kind of clothes Dr. and Mrs. Burney wore. The gentleman is wearing a long cut-away coat which is very fashionable, and he is also wearing a wig. Most gentlemen wore wigs. At the beginning of the eighteenth century wigs were rather large, but by the time the Burney family came to town they were smaller, with the hair gathered in a bow and a kind of pigtail at the back.

19

In the drawings below you can see the different styles of wigs. The one in the centre at the top is called a *periwig*, but by the middle of the century these were only worn by scholars or judges or other learned men. A few gentlemen had their own hair dressed in the fashion of the wigs by a barber, while all servants and working men wore their own hair shoulder length.

The three lower wigs were generally powdered with a thick white powder. Powdering made such a mess that in most homes there was a small powder-closet, like a little dressing-room, where this was done.

There were brown and black wigs for daytime use, but nearly everyone was powdered in the evenings.

The ladies, too, had very elaborate hair styles. These hair-styles took a long time to arrange and sometimes they were kept for as long as a fortnight. At night they were wrapped in a thick cloth to preserve them. There is a story that one lady, when she took her hair down, found a nest of mice in it, but I don't know if this is true! The hair was built up over a thick pad and fixed into place with pins. One lady went to a party with a model of a ship fixed on top of her head. Ladies' hair was always thickly powdered too, like the men's.

But Mrs. Burney would not go in for such complicated hair arrangements, and when her girls grew up they would probably only be powdered for special evening parties. But the ladies' clothes were fairly elaborate and they always spent a long time dressing in the mornings.

The men too had quite costly garments in gay colours, but for everyday wear Dr. Burney would probably be dressed like this gentleman:

His coat is red and trimmed with braid, his breeches dark blue. His stockings are white, his shoes and hat black, his wig grey, and there is some fine lace, probably from Brussels, both on the front of his shirt and showing beyond the cuffs of his coat.

Their home

I expect that when they arrived in London, the Burney children were full of excitement about their new home. It was in St. Martin's Street, near the church of St. Martin-in-the-Fields. There was no Trafalgar Square in those days, and even if there had been a square it would not have had this name: can you say why? A few years before the Burneys settled in, their house was the home of Sir Isaac Newton: do you know why he was famous? The Burney's house is no longer there and now the Westminster City library stands where it used to be—but if you are in London and can find this library you will know just where Fanny's house was.

As you can see, the houses are tall and narrow. At the top are the small windows of the attics where the servants slept.

Probably the first thing the Burney children did was to explore their new home. Perhaps Dr. Burney bought some of his furniture from Mr. Thomas Chippendale, who lived in St. Martin's Lane (and was buried in St. Martin-in-the-Fields). Mr. Chippendale made very dainty and elegant chairs and tables with a higher polish and slimmer legs than had been the fashion. He made sofas and couches covered with silks and satins to match curtains and other draperies, so perhaps Mrs. Burney persuaded her husband to buy a couch and chairs from him for her drawing-room. Below you see the sort of sideboard and chairs there would be in the dining-room:

As well as the dining-room and drawing-room, there would probably be on the ground floor a small study for Dr. Burney where he played upon the *harpsichord* and gave music lessons. The kitchens, store-rooms, and larders would occupy the rest of the ground floor and the basement. Mrs. Burney probably had a china-cupboard where she kept all her best china, for eighteenth-century ladies were very proud of their collections of delicate china. She may even have had a small brewery, for a good deal of beer and ale was still brewed at home.

She certainly had a good store cupboard, always kept locked, from which Mrs. Burney would hand out the stores to the cook when they were required. As well as the cook, there were probably two maids, a butler, a coach-man, and a boy who would clean the shoes, run errands, and generally make himself useful. What a lot of servants! They all slept in the attics, except the boy, who had a little bed in a cupboard under the servants' stairs—a second staircase at the back of the house. In those days a maid would receive about £4 or £5 a year and a butler perhaps £8 to £10 a year and his uniform. It doesn't sound very much, does it? But money was worth a lot more then and you must remember, too, that the servant had a place to live and all his food free.

The bedrooms upstairs would be much more comfortable than those of the previous century. The furniture was altogether more delicate and there were more cushions and covers to make the room cosy. Dr. and Mrs. Burney would sleep in a large bed like this one.

Why was this sort of bed called a four-poster?

A *canopy* was held in place by posts at each corner of the bed, and fine hangings of crimson silk could be drawn right round the bed on a cold winter's night. These made it a warm and snug place to sleep, but it must have been very stuffy. But two hundred years ago people did not understand the importance of fresh air. They thought the night air was harmful, so they drew curtains round their beds, and made sure that every window was tightly closed. Fanny and her sisters may have shared beds such as these, or they may have had low wooden beds without curtains of a sort often used for children and servants.

There was no bathroom in the house, but there was a wash-stand in each bedroom and the maids had to carry jugs of water up the stairs every day for the family's use. When anyone wanted a bath—which was not very often—a movable bath would be placed in front of the fire in their bedroom and filled with jugs of hot water carried up from the kitchen. It involved a great deal of fetching and carrying, and is one reason why no one bothered to bathe as often as we do now when we can just turn on a tap.

Proper fire-grates, like this one, were first introduced in Queen Anne's reign at the beginning of the century; they

were a great improvement on the old open hearth and helped to make the drawing-rooms more elegant. On the floor, Mrs. Burney may have had a carpet made by the factory at Wilton, which was started in 1745 and is still a flourishing business.

Seven o'clock would be the usual hour for rising in the Burney household and a good many jobs were done before breakfast. Dr. Burney would probably have been already at work in his study, while his wife saw to the stores and ordered the day's meals. Probably the older children had done some of their lessons while the younger ones played in the garden. Breakfast was served about ten o'clock and was a light meal of toast and coffee or tea, though probably the children had plenty of bread and butter and perhaps an egg. Dinner, which at the beginning of the century had been served about midday, was gradually becoming later and later, until at this time it was eaten between two and three o'clock in the afternoon. Some of the very fashionable society of London had their dinner at five or six in the evening, but perhaps this was because they often stayed out dancing or at card parties until the early hours of the morning and then did not rise until ten or eleven o'clock in the morning!

What did the family eat for dinner? I think people in the eighteenth century ate a great deal more than we do now. For one dinner they would serve roast beef, roast pork, chicken, veal and ham pies, fish, tarts, cheese, puddings, and fruit. Can you imagine eating that meal? A certain Parson Woodforde kept a diary that gives us a very good idea of life in his time. He says that for five guests he provided "Ham, three fowls boiled, a plum pudding, a couple of ducks roasted, a roasted neck of pork, a plum tart and an apple tart, pears, apples and nuts, wine, beer and cider." They had this meal at four o'clock, followed by tea and coffee, and then at ten o'clock, in case the guests should be hungry before going home, the parson served "hashed fowl, and duck, eggs and potatoes!" What appetites they must have had!

Perhaps the Burneys kept their everyday dinner a little simpler, but they would certainly serve dinners like this whenever they had guests, which was fairly often.

As the dinner hour was so late there was no real afternoon tea as we know it. Tea was served after dinner, but in Fanny's day it was still something of a novelty and everyone loved to drink it—even the poor people would save their money to buy tea, which cost from twelve to sixteen shillings a pound.

Morning callers were given coffee or a glass of wine with cake or biscuits. Coffee was then cheaper than tea and cost only four and sixpence to five shillings a pound. Both coffee and tea were smuggled into the country, with brandy and other spirits, and many people bought these smuggled goods to save paying the heavy taxes imposed by the Customs.

Food was cheap in hotels and inns. Good, solid meals of meat, vegetables and puddings were served, varying in price from one shilling to five shillings. Everybody drank wine and beer, and the poor people in London drank so much bad gin that the Government tried to shut the cheap gin-shops that were ruining people's healths.

As you can see, there was plenty of food and drink, and even the very poor managed to eat quite well, for meat was only twopence or threepence a pound, cheese twopence, and butter round about sixpence. As long as a man was working his family ate well.

Below is a copy of a picture by John Zoffany, a famous artist of this period who lived by the river in Chiswick, where you can still see his house along the part of the towpath called Strand-on-the-green. It is a portrait of a tutor and his young pupil.

Most boys and girls of well-to-do parents had a tutor or governess to teach them at home, and I expect Dr. Burney employed a tutor for his two boys, though no doubt he himself taught them music and perhaps other subjects as well. If parents sent their boys to school at all, they sent them to Eton, Winchester, or Westminster. There is a record of one boy's fees at Westminster School amounting to over sixty pounds a year—a lot of money in those days. Boys did not go to these big schools until about thirteen or fourteen; four years or so later they might go on to Oxford or Cambridge University. Young Charles Burney went to Cambridge, where he proved himself a brilliant scholar, but James entered the Navy when he was fourteen and soon was off to sea with Captain Cook.

The Burney girls had a governess to teach them history, geography, French and simple arithmetic. They would also learn to paint and draw—every girl was supposed to be able to sketch a little—and they also learned sewing and embroidery. Here is a picture of an eighteenth-century *sampler* such as Fanny Burney might have made during her sewing lessons:

It would need a great deal of patience and very neat stitches, wouldn't it? If you go to the Victoria and Albert Museum in London, you can see samplers of this kind made by eighteenth- and nineteenth-century children

Some girls were sent to finishing schools, just as some boys were sent with their tutors on the Grand Tour of Europe, in order to widen their knowledge and give them an idea of how other people lived. But it was only the really wealthy who did this. Most well-to-do families were content if their sons went to Oxford or Cambridge, and if their daughters were charming and accomplished, able to play and sing, dance, sew and draw. Certainly, from all accounts, the Burney girls could do all these things, and the whole family was considered delightful company and was asked out a great deal in fashionable London. When she grew up Fanny held a post at Court, which shows that she grew into a charming and cultured lady—but you will read more about this later on.

For the very poor children there were charity schools, many of which were founded by the Society for the Promotion of Christian Knowledge, a society that still exists today. But many poor parents preferred to send even the little children out to work to earn a few shillings. Some poor children, however, many of them orphans, did go to these charity schools, where they learned to read a little, say their *Catechism*, and do useful work with their hands. These schools were not always very happy places and there were not nearly so many games and interesting things to do as there are in your school today.

Going to Church

All respectable people went to church on Sunday. Sunday was kept as a day of devotion on which as little work was done as possible. The children had to learn their Catechism and verses from the Bible and go with their parents to church. Below you can see a picture by William Hogarth—a very great eighteenth-century artist whose pictures have helped us to understand the manners and customs of his times.

This picture shows morning service in a London church:

Fanny Burney and her family probably attended St. Martin-in-the-Fields' Church, as it was only a few minutes' walk from their house. It had been rebuilt by James Gibbs, a fine architect, and completed in 1726, so the decorations would still be new and fresh when Fanny attended there.

In those days the sermons were very long. They lasted anything from one to three hours, and were sometimes very dull and too difficult for a child to understand. One eighteenth-century sermon lasted nearly four hours! Some of the wealthy gentlemen who attended church arranged for their servants to bring them wine and other refreshments during the sermon. We should think this rather irreverent in church, but when you think how long the services were, it is easy to understand how these gentlemen felt. I think the children must have got very tired too, and in several diaries people write of having fallen asleep during the sermon. But they seldom came late or left early.

The picture is very like the inside of St. Martin-in-the-Fields and you can imagine Fanny and her family here. The box-like pews can still be seen in this church in the gallery and round the sides in the main part of the church. Many fine churches were built in London before and during this period, similar in style to St. Martin's, with wide porches and pillars supporting them, beautiful vaulted ceilings decorated in white and gold or blue, and with smooth polished woodwork. A master mason would be employed to sculpture angels or cherubs where required.

St. Martin's was given a fine organ by George I: he was the first church-warden of the new church. If you live in London or visit it, you must go to this church; you can see a bust of the architect and the wooden model he used when he designed the church.

Two hundred years ago people were beginning to start Sunday schools for poor children. Fanny Burney writes in her diary of one school which she visited in 1791:

Such a number of poor innocent children all put in the way of right; most taken immediately from every way of wrong, lifting their little hands in these prayers and supplications for mercy and grace, which, even if they understand not, must at least impress them with a general idea of religion, a dread of evil, and a love of good.

People of the eighteenth century believed in their church, and were seldom absent on Sundays, and they tried to teach the ignorant so that the children might grow up to be good Christians.

Here is a picture of St. Martin's at about this time:

Can you picture the Burney family walking up the steps into the porch on a fine Sunday morning?

FAMOUS VISITORS IN ST. MARTIN'S STREET

As Fanny Burney grew up, of course, she took more and more part in the family's social life. She was always shy but she did enjoy company, and she loved to listen to clever people talking. In the London of her day there lived a great many men of letters, writers, poets and *playwrights*. There were, too, fine artists and clever architects and decorators. Some of these people were friends of Dr. Burney and his family and often visited their house in St. Martin's Street. So if we look at the visitors who called there we shall meet some of the great men of the time. We can find out who they were by reading the diary Fanny kept.

Her day was no doubt a busy one. As she grew older she would help her mother with some of the household duties—seeing to the stores and ordering the food. She would go out shopping and visiting friends, and some of the day would be occupied with sewing of all kinds. She would also practise her music, for her father liked all his children to be able to play well. In the evening she would help entertain their guests or drive out with her parents to dine with friends, or attend the theatre.

But in spite of her busy life she began in her teens to keep a diary. In it she wrote down not only the things that happened to her, but also some of the conversations she heard, and she gave descriptions of famous people. She must have had a good and careful memory.

So her diary tells us a great deal about her own life and about the lives of famous men and women. She tells us quite a lot about the King and Queen, for instance, as you will read later.

Perhaps the most important man in London society in those days was Dr. Samuel Johnson. We can tell from

35

Fanny's diary that she admired him tremendously. He was very witty but sometimes rather rude to people he considered silly. He was much sought after as a guest at dinner parties because he could be so entertaining.

Samuel Johnson was the son of a Lichfield bookseller, and you can still see his house near the market-square in Lichfield. After leaving Oxford University he came to London. He was very poor and for many years only just managed to scrape a living as a writer. Soon he started work on his English Dictionary. This was the first dictionary of our language, and it took him seven years to complete; when it was published he was paid over fifteen hundred pounds. By now he was becoming famous and his days of poverty were past. In the picture below you can see Dr. Johnson at the *Mitre* tavern in Fleet Street. Opposite him is Oliver Goldsmith, another great writer: do you know his famous book the VICAR OF WAKEFIELD? In the centre is James Boswell, who wrote a *biography* of Dr. Johnson which gives us a wonderful picture of London life at this time.

In spite of his blunt manners and occasional rudeness, 'the doctor' was a very kind man and took into his house several poor and unfortunate people, for he believed he should try and carry out his great faith in the Christian way of life. He lived in several different houses in London; here is one of them:

In her diary Fanny Burney recalls an occasion when Dr. Johnson, as usual, came last into the library; he was in high spirits and full of mirth and sport. I had the honour of sitting next to him. He almost took me in his arms, that is, one of his arms, for one would go three times at least round me, and half-laughing, half serious, he charged me to be a good girl.

Dr. Johnson admired Fanny's book EVELINA and he was a great friend of her father. Johnson's face seemed to light up when talking to the Burneys, so that a friend once exclaimed that Sir Joshua Reynolds should have painted him when he was talking to Dr. Burney or Fanny.

Sir Joshua lived only a short distance away from the Burneys, in Leicester Square. He was a very great portrait painter and if you can go to the National Gallery in London you will see some of his pictures there—if not, see if you can find any copies of his pictures at your school or library or in books about the period. He painted many of the famous people in London, and of him Miss Burney said:

> Sir Joshua I am much pleased with; I like his *countenance* and I like his manners; the former I think expressive, soft and sensible; the latter gentle, unassuming and engaging.

I think it would be nice to have one's picture painted by such a kindly man, don't you?

Another great man of letters whom Fanny knew was Horace Walpole, a great wit and a very elegant gentleman. He was both a writer and a designer. Here is an elaborate staircase he designed for a country house in Twickenham.

One of the most famous playwrights of the day was Richard Brinsley Sheridan, a brilliant Irishman, who always seemed to be in debt, however many successes he had in the theatre. He wrote three well-known plays, THE SCHOOL FOR SCANDAL, THE RIVALS and THE CRITIC. He managed Drury Lane Theatre and when it caught fire he went to watch it burn. A friend could not understand how he could do this, and Sheridan replied: "Why, may a man not sit by his own fireside?"

Here is what Fanny Burney says of him:

Mr. Sheridan has a very fine figure and a good though I don't think a handsome face. He is tall and very upright, and his appearance and dress are at once manly and fashionable without the smallest *tincture* of *foppery* or modish graces. In short, I like him vastly.

The leading actor in most of Sheridan's plays was David Garrick, one of the most celebrated actors of all time. This is a sketch of him:

Everybody in London wanted to meet David Garrick after seeing him act. Charlotte Burney, Fanny's sister, once wrote in her diary that Garrick recognized them at the theatre. I expect he, too, had enjoyed his visits to St. Martin's Street, for he seemed very pleased to see the Burney girls and shook hands with them all. Susan Burney said how proud they were to meet him, and Charlotte put in her diary that she would "a hundred times rather be spoken to by Garrick in public than His Majesty the King!"

Another famous man whom Fanny Burney met was Edmund Burke. He was a Member of Parliament and a great prose writer and he loved liberty and justice above all things. Most of his ideas were too advanced for the people of his day, for he saw all mankind as one great family and believed that everyone was born with certain rights and duties and must be respected as an individual.

This is what Fanny Burney wrote about Edmund Burke in her diary:

> He is tall, his figure noble, his air commanding. His voice is clear and penetrating, *sonorous* and powerful. His manners are attractive, his conversation delightful.

Here is a picture copied from an artist's drawing of many of these famous people sitting down to dinner together:

On the left is Boswell, and I expect you can recognize Dr. Johnson next to him. Sir Joshua Reynolds is next, with his ear trumpet, and next to him is Edmund Burke. Garrick is in the middle. The fat man is an Italian artist, and in front of him is Charles Burney, Fanny's brother. Goldsmith is sitting at the end of the table where another friend is whispering to him.

You will understand from what you have just been reading that this was a time when a great many people were writing books and plays and poems. Until the eighteenth century there was not much choice of books or papers when you wanted to spend an evening reading. On most bookshelves you would find Bunyan's PILGRIM'S PROGRESS, Foxe's BOOK OF MARTYRS, perhaps some essays by Francis Bacon, and a story or poems by Sir Philip Sidney. However, during the eighteenth century many new books and magazines were written. GULLIVER'S TRAVELS, by Dean Swift, and ROBINSON CRUSOE, by Daniel Defoe, were published—have you read these two books? I am sure you would enjoy them. Novels were published, too, by Samuel Richardson and Henry Fielding, and became very popular. Joseph Addison and Richard Steele wrote a magazine together; it was called THE SPECTATOR, and later there was another called THE TATLER. These were the earliest kind of magazines, but they were not in the least like our gay coloured magazines, and I'm afraid you might find them rather dull. Addison also wrote a series of articles, later put together in a book called SIR ROGER DE COVERLEY, the amusing story of a kindly country *squire*.

You can see that by the end of the eighteenth century there was much more to read. A great many people, however, never bothered to read at all, and many could not read. But there were plenty of amusements both for rich and poor.

HOW THE RICH PEOPLE ENJOYED THEMSELVES

Most of the people in what we call 'Society' were people with titles or who belonged to some of the great families of England. They got their income from their property, land and *tenants*, and many of them took a great interest in their estates and cared for them seriously. But when in London, their time was spent in enjoyment. There were, of course, exceptions to this rule, such as those who were in Parliament, those who were Justices of the Peace, and others who held posts at Court.

London Society lived mainly in the area which we now call Mayfair—Grosvenor Square, Hanover Square, Portman and Cavendish Squares, Curzon Street, and Half Moon Street. In the picture below you see Hanover Square with St. George's Church in the background. This church is still a great place for fashionable weddings. Do you see the elegant carriage in which the lady and gentleman are driving? This was called a *phaeton*, and used a

great deal in pleasant weather, but if it rained the ladies got very wet.

For most of their visiting the wealthy people used a *chaise*, or a slightly larger type of carriage similar to this:

If a lady or gentleman was going visiting alone, he or she very often used a sedan chair. Do you remember seeing a picture of some of these when we took our first walk round the town? Ladies used this kind of conveyance a great deal as they were cheap and easy to use, though of course slower than a carriage drawn by horses. When a lady returned from a ball or a card-party at night, she would be carried home in a sedan chair like this one:

In this kind of conveyance a lady would be safe enough from thieves and pickpockets, of which there were plenty lurking in the streets. But gentlemen who rode or drove out with their families to houses outside the town for an evening's entertainment had always to be on the watch for highwaymen. Hounslow Heath and Hampstead were places where these rogues often held up coaches and stole the money from the men and jewels from the ladies. Some highwaymen were just ignorant criminals, but a few were gentlemen who, for one reason or another, 'took to the road' to make some money. Some were quite gay with their victims, and there is a story of one gentleman-highwayman who danced a *quadrille* with a lady before stealing her pearls! Most people who travelled far carried pistols, and no gentleman went out at night in town without his sword, even if it was only a light dress sword.

Let us see what sort of entertainment there was for the rich. Many of them had beautiful homes to which they invited their friends. Two brothers, Robert and James Adam, were at this time designing houses with fine rooms, containing elegant fireplaces of carved marble, ornate ceilings and walls covered with silk or *taffeta* or pretty striped paper. There was often a window above the front door of a house designed by them: it was shaped like a fan and called a fanlight. You can see one in the picture on page 56 of Boodle's Club, which was designed by the Adam brothers.

On the next page is a cross-section of a house designed by Robert Adam. You can see that the outside steps lead into an elaborate hall with a high, domed ceiling, and beyond is a pillared room used probably as a ballroom or dining-hall. You can see that the people of those times were fond of carving and of marble statues.

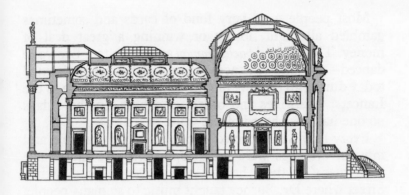

And here is another room of the kind in which people entertained their friends to cards or music or dancing:

Most people were very fond of cards and sometimes gambled all night, losing or winning a great deal of money. They played *backgammon* and chess too. Everyone danced—the kind of dances you sometimes see performed today during an evening of Old Time dancing, such as the Lancers, quadrilles and other set dances. In those days no one had ever heard of the waltz or foxtrot.

Every lady was expected to be able to play or sing, and musical evenings were very popular. There must have been many of these held at the house in St. Martin's Street where Dr. Burney taught music to so many people. Below you can see a concert ticket designed by the artist, William Hogarth, who lived close to the Burneys and to Sir Joshua Reynolds, in Leicester Square. It shows the sort of instruments used:

Mary's Chappel   Five at Night

Concerts were given in private houses and also in public halls and in the pleasure gardens. Handel was the most famous composer of this time. I expect you know some of his music. Probably you have heard the music composed by him for the Royal Fireworks display, or the Water Music composed for the King to listen to one summer evening in his barge on the River Thames. Perhaps you have heard Handel's famous oratorio MESSIAH sung at Christmas-time. An oratorio is a sacred story set to music; it requires soloists, a choir and an orchestra, but there are no costumes or scenery or acting. Handel was a very great and a good man and when he wrote his wonderful music for MESSIAH—the story of the birth and life of Jesus—he believed that he was inspired by God.

Another composer writing delightful music was Dr. Arne. He set several of Shakespeare's songs to music, and he also wrote one song which you all know—'Rule, Britannia!'

Here is a playbill announcing a performance of COMUS, a masque by John Milton, to be given at the Theatre Royal in Drury Lane.

Do you notice that Mrs. Arne is to take part? The bill also warns you not to be late—do you see that it says it is to begin at exactly six o'clock? I expect the people who came late were very unpopular.

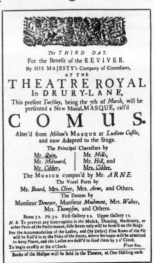

The *THIRD DAY*.
For the Benefit of the R E V I V E R.
By HIS MAJESTY's Company of Comedians,
AT THE
T H E A T R E R O Y A L
In D R U R Y - L A N E,
This present *Tuesday*, being the 7th of *March*, will be presented a New Moral, MASQUE, call'd
C O M U S.
Alter'd from *Milton*'s MASQUE at *Ludlow Caſtle*, and now Adapted to the Stage.
The Principal Characters by

Mr. *Quin*,	Mr. *Mills*,
Mr. *Milward*,	Mr. *Hill*, and
Mr. *Cibber*,	Mrs. *Cibber*,

The MUSICK compos'd by Mr. *ARNE*.
The Vocal Parts by
Mr. *Beard*, Mrs. *Clive*, Mrs. *Arne*, and Others.
The Dances by
Monſieur *Denoyer*, Monſieur *Muilment*, Mrs. *Walter*, Mrs. *Thompſon*, and Others.

Boxes 5 s. Pit 3 s. Firſt Gallery 2 s. Upper Gallery 1 s.
N. B. To prevent any Interruption in the Muſick, Dancing, Machinery, or other Parts of the Performance, Side Boxes only will be form'd on the Stage. For the Accommodation of the Ladies, and (by Deſire) Five Rows of the Pit will be Rail'd in at the Price of the Boxes, where Servants will be admitted to keep Places, and the Ladies are deſir'd to ſend them by 3 o'Clock.
To begin exactly at Six o'Clock. *Vivat Rex.*
Books of the Maſque will be Sold in the Theatre, at One Shilling each.

47

There was a musical play first performed in 1728 which is still very popular today. This was THE BEGGAR'S OPERA. It was written by John Gay, a poet and composer of light songs, who made up the musical score from many old folk tunes that might otherwise have been forgotten. It is very tuneful music and the composer's name tells you what it is like! If you get a chance to see this light opera, I think you will enjoy it very much—it is all about a highwayman.

There were two big theatres in London then, Covent Garden Opera House, and the Theatre Royal, Drury Lane. Both are still in use and are two of the best theatres in London. I think you would be rather surprised at the way the audience behaved if you had gone to the theatre in the eighteenth century. Important people who went to the theatre were allowed to sit on the stage itself, and there were boxes alongside it so that the actors had their audience on three sides of their stages. If the play proved unpopular the young men in the audience would sometimes rush up on to the stage with their swords drawn and wreck the scenery and stage furnishings. In this picture you can see such a riot beginning:

Tickets for the boxes and pit cost five shillings, those for the gallery two shillings, and only one shilling for the upper gallery. During the eighteenth century, however, the conditions in the theatres improved, the audience were removed from the stage, which gradually took the shape we see now instead of jutting out into the main part of the theatre as it used to do. There were a good many famous actors during this time, among them John Rich, Colley Cibber, and Charles Macklin, while towards the end of the century all London was flocking to see Mrs. Sarah Siddons. But the greatest of them all was David Garrick, who did much to improve the conditions in the theatre and who brought a fine type of acting to it. He was a great dramatic actor, and a good *comedian*, but he seldom over-acted as so many others did. He played in Shakespeare's plays and made the characters come alive, and he acted too in the plays by Richard Brinsley Sheridan—do you remember meeting him earlier in this book when he visited the Burney family? He acted too in another play still acted today—SHE STOOPS TO CONQUER. This play was by Oliver Goldsmith: do you remember meeting him at the *Mitre* tavern with Dr. Johnson?

David Garrick also invented the system of lighting the stage by footlights and added other improvements to his theatre; he was a great friend of Dr. Johnson and he was treated with great affection and respect in London society.

Now, let us pretend it is a summer evening in June two hundred years ago. You and I are going out to enjoy ourselves. As it is rather hot, we will not go to the theatre; instead we will visit some of the lovely pleasure-gardens which Londoners all enjoyed. I think first of all we will go to Vauxhall by the river. We enter a spacious garden laid out in delightful cool walks paved with gravel and bordered by hedges and trees. Here and there are pavilions and *grottoes*, pillars and statues; everywhere lanterns made to look like suns and moons and stars are hanging in the trees, and the whole place is decorated like a kind of fairyland. In the different pavilions we can buy wine or tea and all kinds of cold food, prettily decorated little cakes or cold meats as we fancy.

As we walk through this fairyland and see the moon rising through the trees and watch the lamps swaying in the gentle breeze we can hear the sound of music. Shall we go into the music-room and listen? This room is a large round hall, richly carved and decorated, and an orchestra and singers are performing some songs by Dr. Arne. We will sit on a bench by the wall and listen.

Here is a picture of the music-room at Vauxhall:

Do you notice the beautifully decorated ceiling? What does it look like?

The ladies and gentlemen passing by us are dressed in a variety of colours, so that the room is gay with blue and pink and yellow taffetas, purple and scarlet and green and brown silks and velvets. As well as the wealthy people, there are more soberly dressed merchants, clerks, and lawyers out with their families for the evening.

Now we will walk down the central path between the trees and towards an ornate arch—you can see in this picture just where we are going. Do you notice the statues? At the end we will stop to drink a cup of tea and eat some of the pretty iced cakes at one of the many refreshment stalls.

Now we will take a boat up the river from Lambeth stairs, where there is a horse ferry. Can you find Horseferry Road on a map of London? We get off at Ranelagh Gardens. These gardens are now part of the grounds of Chelsea Hospital, for old and disabled soldiers—have you ever seen Chelsea Pensioners walking about in their scarlet coats and black hats and trousers? Dr. Burney was the organist at Chelsea Hospital for the last twenty-seven years of his life, and was buried here.

But on our hot night in June in 1760 the Ranelagh Gardens have nothing to do with the Hospital and are gay with coloured lights. For the fashionable ladies and gentlemen of London, the Rotunda is a particular attraction. This is a large circular building which, when lit up at night, is called 'The Giant's Lantern'. Inside it there are rows of gaily-coloured boxes where we can eat and drink while we listen to the orchestra playing in the centre of the building. The place is lighted by *chandeliers* of candles burning in crystal cases, and they twinkle like thousands of stars. This is what the Rotunda looks like from the outside:

Often there are masked balls held here, and these are quite exciting, because it is fun to guess who people are when their faces are hidden by black velvet masks. At midnight these are taken off and it is quite surprising to find you have been talking to a complete stranger when you thought it was Cousin Susan! Walking down the paths of the rose garden we may come across Dr. Johnson walking with Mr. Boswell, or Sir Joshua Reynolds, or the great David Garrick.

Another evening we cross Oxford Street to the fields of St. Marylebone and visit the Pleasure Gardens there. Duels, though forbidden by law, are sometimes fought in the fields, and highwaymen lurk on the way to the Gardens, but this does not prevent Londoners riding out to these pleasant places in the evenings.

It is also considered very fashionable to drink healing

waters at various springs. There is a spring at Sadler's Wells and I think we must go there and drink the waters in the pretty tea-house. The picture shows what Sadler's Wells looked like.

The spring here was discovered by a surveyor named Sadler in 1683, and it costs threepence to drink the waters. There is musical entertainment as well as tightrope walkers, jugglers and clowns to watch. Nowadays Sadler's Wells is famous for its theatre, and its ballet company is known all over the world.

Coffee Houses and Clubs

Ladies occupied themselves a great deal with visiting and shopping in Cheapside and other places in the City—there were no 'West End' shops then. They also liked to play cards. The gentlemen, however, spent most of their time at coffee-houses or clubs.

At this time there were nearly three thousand coffee-houses in London, so you can tell how popular they were. They were places where gentlemen met to talk and listen to great men. Poets and playwrights were known to go to certain houses and their admirers flocked there to listen to them. Noblemen mixed with other men, and all drank coffee together, read the papers, discussed art, politics, religion and literature.

Some of these coffee-houses had very strange names—THE TILTYARD, THE CHAPTER, THE COCOA TREE, THE SMYRNA, BUTTON'S, and THE TURK'S HEAD are just a few. Here is a picture of a coffee-house:

You can see the girl at the counter serving the coffee, which attendants take round while the gentlemen sit and talk. I can see one man smoking a pipe, but this was not encouraged in most coffee-houses; on the whole the gentlemen preferred taking snuff. Snuff was a kind of sneezing powder and it was carried in little boxes which fitted into a man's coat pocket; a pinch of snuff would make him sneeze several times and people thought that this cleared the head.

In the picture you can also see a large urn of water heating over the fire. Do you notice that they are using small cups without saucers?

Many merchants did a good deal of their business in the coffee-houses in the City. Have you heard of the famous business that insures ships and their cargoes—Lloyd's? Well, that was started by a man named Edward Lloyd in a coffee-house where men interested in ships used to meet together. THE CHAPTER COFFEE-HOUSE in Paternoster Row was particularly famous for meetings of booksellers who here bought and sold their books; young men would go to this house of small low-ceilinged rooms in search of work as writers, and it gradually became the favourite resort of those who wanted to know what was going on in the world of letters. Oliver Goldsmith or Dr. Johnson often went there, perhaps with a man named Longman who owned a bookshop nearby and also published books—as his descendants have published this book two hundred years later.

There were many coffee-houses too in the 'West End'. Dr. Johnson and Oliver Goldsmith both used to go to the ST. JAMES'S coffee-house, and 'The Doctor' also liked THE TURK'S HEAD, and PEELE'S; the poets, John Dryden and Alexander Pope, went to WILL'S; Hogarth was fond of THE BEDFORD. Anyone who wanted to hear any of these famous people talk went to one of these coffee-houses, where they were generally to be found surrounded by an admiring audience.

At SLAUGHTER'S one could meet men from the artistic world. Sir Joshua Reynolds would be there, and other famous artists such as George Romney and Thomas Gainsborough, and of course William Hogarth, who has given us such a clear idea of what the London of his day was like. Here is a picture he painted of himself with his dog:

As well as coffee-houses, men had their clubs. The very famous BEEF-STEAK CLUB in Fleet Street was founded by George Lambert, an artist, and Hogarth's name is second on the list of members; Dr. Johnson was a member, as well as David Garrick and Henry Fielding, who was a Justice of the Peace and who also wrote novels. WHITE'S was a well-known club where there was a great deal of gambling. The KIT-KAT was famous for having the highest nobility in the land among its members. It was originally founded for political reasons, that is, by men who were loyal to George I in troubled times and who wished to form themselves into a strong party to support him.

The COCOA TREE CLUB was formed to support the exiled Stuarts, James II and later James III and Bonny Prince Charlie, and to oppose the KIT-KAT CLUB. Here is a picture of BOODLE'S CLUB, which you can still see in St. James's Street:

ALMACK'S was another thriving club at which there was a good deal of card-playing. A private letter written in 1770 says that

the young men of the age lose ten, fifteen, twenty thousand pounds in an evening there. Lord Stavordale, not one-and-twenty, lost £11,000 there last Tuesday, but recovered it by one great hand at Hazard.

What a lot of money to win or lose! In those days there were both more very rich men and more very poor men than there are nowadays when money is more evenly spread among the people of this country.

BROOKS'S CLUB 'for gentlemen of good family' is, like WHITE'S and BOODLE'S, still running as a club today.

Dr. Johnson founded the LITERARY CLUB. Edmund Burke and Sir Joshua Reynolds were among its members and Dr. Burney, our old friend, was at one time its Treasurer.

Most of these clubs met in taverns. You have read earlier in this book of the many taverns in London and of the strange names some of them had. They served as restaurants, too. Most people in those days dined out a great deal, especially those gentlemen who lived in lodgings. Many taverns, such as the CHESHIRE CHEESE in Fleet Street, were famous for the excellent food they served.

So you see that coffee-houses, clubs and taverns, theatres and concerts, pleasure gardens and spas, as well as private entertainments, provided plenty of ways for the rich people to entertain themselves, and even those less well off were able to join in some of the fun.

Now we must find out how the humbler people lived. We will visit first a shopkeeper's family.

LIFE IN THE HOUSE OF
ROBERT GIBBON, DRAPER

Robert Gibbon was the grandfather of the historian Edward Gibbon, who wrote a very long and famous book about THE DECLINE AND FALL OF THE ROMAN EMPIRE. Robert kept a draper's shop in Ludgate Hill below St. Paul's Cathedral. Here is a picture by William Hogarth to give you some idea of what the inside of a shop looked like. You can see all the shelves for materials.

Hogarth drew this picture for shop-bills which his own sisters used in their shop, but Mr. Gibbon's shop was probably very like this.

Mr. Gibbon lived above and behind his shop, and the household consisted of himself and his wife, two sons, a maid, and one or two *apprentices*. The family would be up early, for the shop opened at eight o'clock. The apprentices, boys between twelve and perhaps twenty-one years of age, would take down the shutters and busy themselves setting out the stock. During the morning the customers would be mainly City gentlemen, for the ladies seldom did their shopping before the afternoon. So, while Robert attended to the business and did the accounts, his wife would order the day's food and supervise the housework. She also made pickles, wines and *cordials*, as well as all kinds of jams and *chutneys*. All kinds of fruit and vegetables were preserved, and a City housewife was very proud of her store-cupboard.

Breakfast probably consisted of cold meat and beer Dinner was served at about two o'clock when the family ate an excellent meal during which they were waited on by the apprentices, who ate their own meal afterwards. Business in the shop continued through the afternoon. Here is an account of a visit to a draper's shop which was written in the eighteenth century.

> The shops are perfect gilded theatres, the variety of silks like so many changes in fine scenes. As people glance within their doors, the shopkeepers salute them with "Garden silks, ladies; Italian silks; Geneva silks; fine thread satins, both striped and plain; mohair silks; Norwich crepes; silks for hoods and scarves, and right Scottish plaids."

There seems to have been a good selection of materials!

Here is a picture of the front of a shop in Artillery Row, Houndsditch:

And here is one of an arcade of shops:

These two pictures will give you an idea of what the shops two hundred years ago were like. According to all accounts written at the time, they seem to have been very busy, and the ladies loved shopping then as much as they do now! The prices were not so clearly fixed as they are now and everyone argued or bargained about what to pay for a yard of cloth. A good silk would cost about twelve or thirteen shillings a yard.

Here is a list of some of the things which a draper sold and the prices he charged. Compare these with today's prices when you next visit a big store.

	£	s.	d.
Kid gloves		2	6
Cambric handkerchief		10	0
Shoes		2 10	0
Silk stockings	1	0	0
Table cloths		8	0
Muslin, per yard		7	0
Irish linen, per yard—from		4	6
—to		7	6
French dress	3	0	0
Imitation flowers	2	0	0

The flowers to wear in the hair seem very expensive, for instance, while the gloves are really very cheap.

In the evening the draper would go to a tavern or coffee-house to meet his friends, and he would probably choose a place where other drapers were to be found and business could be discussed. Merchants and tradesmen had their clubs as well as the richer people. There was, for example, a Sixpenny Card Club at the Queen's Arms in St. Paul's Churchyard—this does not, of course, mean in the churchyard itself, but in the lane running round the Cathedral on the north side. Apprentices, having little or no money to spend, would run wild in the streets during the evenings, and generally get into mischief.

Mrs. Gibbon would probably entertain her friends to supper and a small card-party, where they gossiped about city affairs. Sometimes she and her husband would sup with friends, for the people of this time were very fond of parties of all kinds.

There were academies for boys and girls of the tradesmen's families, and Mr. Gibbon sent his sons to one of these schools, where they would learn writing, arithmetic, Latin, and probably some French. They would also learn their Catechism and study the Bible. The two boys must have learned their lessons well, for one became Dean of Carlisle and the other a Commissioner of Customs, a man responsible for seeing that the correct sums of money were taken by Government officials on goods coming into the country.

The family would dress in the same kind of clothes as I described when we were visiting Fanny Burney and her family. The Gibbons' dress would be rather plainer, of course, especially during the week, but they would all dress up on Sundays and go to church.

Perhaps twice a year they would go to Vauxhall Pleasure Gardens as a family outing, or for a trip down the river, and they would visit Southwark Fair, which was held once a year. But for the most part the family entertained itself among friends and there was not the time or money for much theatre-going or the other enjoyments of the more wealthy.

Now let us find out how much it cost the Gibbon family to live, how much they spent every week on the ordinary things of life.

Here is a list of their weekly expenses:

	£	s.	d.
Bread		5	4
Butter (1 lb. per day)		5	3
Cheese (3½ lb.)		1	5½
Roots, herbs and spices			6
Meat, fish and fowl	1	8	0
Eggs (4d.), Flour (1s. 2d.)		1	6
12 gallons small beer		4	8
Tea (2s.), Sugar (3s.)		5	0
Candles 4 lb.		3	0
Coals (2 fires in winter, 1 in summer: weekly average)		5	6
Soap, blue, starch, etc.		5	0
Thread, needles, tape, etc.		1	9
Sand, *fuller's earth*, whitening, scouring paper, brick dust, etc.			4
Repairs to furniture, etc.		2	0
	£3	9	3½

As well as the weekly expenses, Mr. Gibbon would probably allow about £60 a year for clothing for himself, his wife and children, £8 for schooling, £5 for medicines and the doctor's bills, about £15 for wages, £66 for rent and taxes, £20 for entertainments for his friends, and another £10 for wine and other sundries. In all, his income needed to be about £400 a year.

As you can see, there is no allowance for holidays. The London tradesmen seldom left their homes and shops, except for an occasional visit to a relative.

I don't suppose the family lit more than one candle at a time in the evenings, except when they had guests, and the allowance of 4 lb. for the week, though it may seem a lot to you, would not be enough for them to burn more than about two a day in the parlour and one in the kitchen.

Rents varied from £50 a year to £150 for a good house round St. Paul's, in Cheapside, or towards Bloomsbury. Houses were taxed, too—the rate varying from 6d. to 1s. in the £—and there was also a window-tax, 2d. for every window. Have you ever seen an old house with some of the windows blocked in? This was done in order to avoid paying this tax, for in some big houses it would become quite expensive. In a house with twenty-three windows, how much tax would the owner have to pay? Of course most houses in the City only had about twelve to sixteen windows.

The labourer, however, did not live nearly so well. A man who worked as a coal-heaver or a dock-worker had to manage on 15s. to £1 a week. They lived in poor houses, paying very little rent, and this is the kind of food they ate:

Breakfast:
  Bread and cheese and small beer.

Dinner:
  Scrag of mutton, or sheep's trotters or pigs' ears.
  Cabbage or potatoes or parsnips.
  Bread and beer.

Supper:
  Bread and cheese with radishes or onions or cucumbers.
  Beer.

It sounds rather a dull diet, doesn't it? On Sundays the working-man might have something extra, and on special occasions the family would have eggs, or puddings, or some other food that they considered a luxury, though we would regard it as quite an ordinary dish.

Working-men depended on merchants and tradesmen such as Mr. Gibbon for their living.

When Mr. Gibbon wanted to buy material for his shop he might go down to the riverside, to the docks where the ships came in from all over the world. Here he could buy Eastern silks and many unusual foreign types of cloth.

Here is a picture of the East India Wharf at London Bridge:

The East India Company was one of the most famous of all trading companies, and they dealt in tea, chinaware, *indigo*, copper, raw silk and silk materials, fans and shawls. From the west came furs, tobacco, sugar, and various kinds of wood for furniture making. So, many merchants would meet at the dockside to buy and bargain and talk business.

Mr. Gibbon would also buy his materials from a weaver who employed craftsmen and labourers in his workshop; here he would get woollen and cotton cloth. Below is a picture of a weaver's workshop—as drawn by Hogarth:

You can see the large and rather clumsy machinery they used. The master is watching the men to see that they do their work properly—one of them is hard at work, while the other is being lazy, which is hardly surprising when you know the long hours they worked.

The usual working day was from six in the morning until seven or eight at night. There was no Saturday half-day and there were no bank holidays—Sunday was the only day of rest for these hard-working folk.

What it was like to be an Apprentice

Tom was one of Mr. Gibbon's apprentices. He was sixteen years old and an orphan. Since he had no parents, he was apprenticed by the parish—that is by the church officers—at the age of twelve when he left the charity school where he had learned to read and write. Ralph, the other apprentice living in Mr. Gibbon's house, was eighteen, and he was apprenticed by his father, a master builder.

Their *indentures*—the legal documents prepared and signed by the father or guardian and by the employer of an apprentice—bound them to learn the trade and serve under Mr. Gibbon until they were twenty-one years old. Employers were paid to take an apprentice. For example, Mr. Gibbon was paid the sum of £30 by Ralph's father. This was to cover Ralph's clothes and his training in the drapery business. In return for this sum and Ralph's services, Mr. Gibbon fed and housed him and for eight or nine years treated the boy as a member of the family. Tom, too, lived as part of the family.

The apprentices' day began very early indeed. On one particularly cold morning they were up at about half-past four or five and after dressing themselves they swept out the shop, laid out materials and made everything tidy for the day's business. They breakfasted off cold meats, bread and beer, and then at half-past seven or eight they took down the heavy sliding shutters, one at the top and one at the bottom of the shop windows. Now the doors were opened and the shop was ready for customers. All London was astir early and many people used to shop before eight in the morning.

Mr. Gibbon came in to see that all was ready; if he

found dust lying about anywhere, he probably spoke severely to Ralph and Tom, telling them that no customer likes to visit a dirty shop. Having a little time to spare, he gave his apprentices a lesson in how to recognize different kinds of cloth, to guess its weight by the feel of it, and how to know a good bargain.

During the morning Ralph served a gentleman with four yards of broadcloth at 16s. 6d. a yard, another with two *Holland* shirts at fifteen shillings each. Tom served one lady with a *damask* table cloth costing 8s., and another with several yards of Irish linen at 5s. 6d. a yard.

Just before dinner, Mrs. Gibbon found she had run out of salt, so she sent Tom hurrying to the nearest grocer. On the way back Tom saw a party of performing jugglers and acrobats, but he ran off when one of them came round with a hat asking for pennies, for Tom's pockets were empty. Home again, he was scolded by Mrs. Gibbon for being so slow, and Mr. Gibbon told him he was a 'lazy good-for-nothing.' The shop closed for the dinner-hour, when the family sat down to a nourishing meal of boiled beef, vegetables and dumplings, with bread and beer. Tom and Ralph waited on the family, wishing that they would hurry up and finish, for the two apprentices were hungry after their morning's work. Soon they were sitting down to plates full of steaming food.

During the afternoon some of the ladies from the more fashionable quarters of London came to the shop to buy silks, and muslins, fans and gloves, and Ralph served one gentleman with a handsome pair of red velvet breeches that cost £2 2s. 0d. Mr. Gibbon was very pleased about this and nodded encouragingly at Ralph. When at last the shop was closed at eight o'clock, both boys were feeling tired, for they had had a long day on their feet and during the afternoon both had had to go out delivering parcels.

But after a supper of bread and cheese and onions, and beer, they felt refreshed and went out into the streets. Tom had no money, but Ralph said he must come with him to enjoy himself. Some apprentices who came from good families like Ralph would have nothing to do with poor parish apprentices like Tom, but Ralph was a kind boy and he took Tom to a tavern where they met their friends to laugh and chatter and play games. Sometimes they ran races in the streets, and sometimes they got into mischief, but usually Ralph and Tom came home before the street lamps were put out, at eleven o'clock.

They had to make up their beds themselves. Ralph had first choice of where to make his bed and he chose to sleep on the counter in the shop. There it was warm and airy; he had blankets and a straw mattress and made quite a comfortable bed. Tom had to sleep in a box-like cupboard under the stairs, where it was very stuffy; there were mice there too. However, he had the same bedding as Ralph and was soon asleep. All too soon it would be five o'clock, and they must begin another day.

Ralph and Tom were lucky, for they worked for a good master who treated them fairly and fed them well—but in eighteenth-century London there were many unjust masters who did not carry out their side of the bargain and who ill-treated their apprentices, using them like slaves. Sometimes apprentices ran away and were severely punished if they were caught.

When they had served their term of apprenticeship they were free to work as *journeymen*, that is as craftsmen working for a master and earning a wage. Or they could, if they had any money, set up in business on their own.

69

To set up a drapery shop would cost about £1,000. A man with a good training could generally join the company or *guild* of his own trade and thus become a '*liveryman*'—that is, entitled to wear the company's uniform.

There were, however, less fortunate people. There were boys employed as chimney-sweeps. If you have read THE WATER BABIES by Charles Kingsley, you will know what an unpleasant life these little boys had. Sold to their masters at the age of five or six, they were forced to climb up inside chimneys and, half-choked with soot, to sweep out the chimney. Little girls worked in factories or as domestic servants and some of them were not at all well treated, for there were no laws then to protect them from having to work for very long hours when still far too young.

There were many unfortunate people who could not find work, and others who did not want to work. There were many beggars in the streets, and some of these made a good living—they even sent their children out to beg. Walking down the Strand, you might be stopped a dozen times by ragged or crippled children begging for pennies. There were many of these destitute children in London. If you read OLIVER TWIST by Charles Dickens, you will get an idea of the sort of life they led. I think it will make you feel glad you are living in the twentieth century.

WHEN YOU WERE ILL

What happens nowadays if you are taken ill? The doctor comes round in his car to see you and he may give you medicine to make you better. If he thinks you ought to go to hospital, a gleaming white ambulance comes to take you there. There are doctors and nurses to look after you in the hospital and everything is beautifully clean. If you have an operation, there is a *surgeon* to do the operation and a man called an anaesthetist to send you into a deep sleep so that you feel no pain. Rich and poor alike receive the best possible medical treatment.

But in the eighteenth century things were very different. For one thing, the doctors did not know a great deal about the human body and how it worked.

The doctors who belonged to the College of *Physicians* considered themselves the most able to help people— they were trained and they asked high fees from their patients.

Next came the *Apothecaries*—we call them chemists— and they *prescribed* cures for different diseases, that is, they treated their customers as a doctor treats his patients and then made up medicines and drugs to try and cure them. The physicians and apothecaries were always quarrelling, as the doctors did not think anyone but themselves should prescribe medicines. The poor people, however, could not afford the doctors' fees and went to the apothecaries when they were sick.

The Surgeons were not considered nearly so important as either the physicians or apothecaries. They belonged to the Company of Barber Surgeons, so that a man might be both a barber and a surgeon at the same time—it seems an odd mixture, doesn't it? In 1745 Surgeons broke away from the Barbers' guild and decided to form their own company; at first they found it very difficult to keep going, for no one had much respect for surgeons, but by 1800 they became known as the Royal College of Surgeons and before much longer were firmly established. In the middle of the eighteenth century, however, they were still only allowed to operate in the presence of a physician and could only prescribe for their patients with the permission of the physician.

At the beginning of the century there were only four hospitals in London, but during the century Guy's, the London, St. George's, Queen Charlotte's and the Middlesex were opened among others. Here is a picture of St. Bartholomew's Hospital, one of the original four:

Thomas Guy, who founded Guy's Hospital in 1721, was a bookseller at Cornhill. He made a fortune on the Stock Exchange and invested most of it, spending very little on himself. In time he became a very rich man and provided the money for the building of the hospital which today we still know as Guy's Hospital. He will always be remembered as a man who made money not for himself but to help the people of his city. Here is a picture of a ward at Guy's Hospital. Notice how the beds are like boxes laid against the wall.

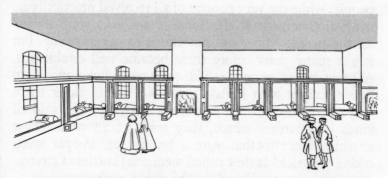

Another man who greatly benefited the city was Captain Thomas Coram, who built a hospital for *foundlings*. In the eighteenth century there were many tramps and beggars. Sometimes these people did not want their babies and left them on doorsteps or near churches so that the parish would bring them up in a charity home. Sometimes these children died of cold or hunger before a home was found for them. Captain Coram was determined to help these little ones, so he built the Foundling Hospital for them. Here it is:

I have told you that the doctors charged high fees for their attendance. Most of them were learned men, and made a great deal of money from their rich patients. It was mainly the apothecaries who looked after the poorer people, while the very poorest of all received practically no medical treatment at all. Some *dispensaries* were started for the people who could not afford to pay anything, but it was many years before these became well established. A great many people relied on women who made up queer recipes with herbs: today we should think them very odd medicines. There were *pedlars*, too, who sold all kinds of mixtures which, they said, would cure almost anything from toothache to a broken leg. People loved taking 'physick' as they called medicine; bottles of strange mixtures always sold well in the street markets.

As the eighteenth century progressed, there was a great advance in medical knowledge. Doctors began to realize how much cleanliness mattered and that disease and dirt were always found together. It was the beginning of the fine medical service we know today, and so we should remember that many of London's famous hospitals, which have brought so many people back to health, were founded by men of vision and compassion who lived in the eighteenth century.

THE LORD MAYOR AND THE
CITY OF LONDON

Nobody is quite certain when the City of London was divided into twenty-six *wards*—even in the eighteenth century this division was ancient. Each ward was represented by its own *alderman* and *common councilmen* who were elected by the *freemen* of the ward. The common councilmen were elected for one year at the time, but the aldermen were elected for life. The Lord Mayor was chosen every year from the twenty-six aldermen, just as he is today.

The Lord Mayor was very powerful and no one could interfere with his rule in the City. Two hundred years ago it had recently been decided that during his year of office the Lord Mayor should live in a special house—and so the Mansion House was built. The first Lord Mayor to live there moved into it in 1753. The Lord Mayor was, and is, the Chief Justice of the City, and each alderman was a Justice in his own ward. There were also two *Sheriffs* of London and Middlesex—they collected fines, attended the judges and carried out their orders, took charge of criminals and saw that executions were carried out.

The less important officers were elected by all the men of the ward, whether they were freemen or not. One of these was the Recorder, a lawyer, who was paid a thousand pounds a year to advise the aldermen on matters to do with the law. There were also bailiffs, clerks, surveyors, stewards, *beadles*, a town crier who made announcements, and a *coroner*. All these men worked at the Guildhall, which was, as it is today, the City of London's town hall.

A City ward was not very big, covering perhaps half-a-dozen streets. Before leaving the City let us visit Tower Ward, for there we shall find the Tower of London, one of London's most famous buildings.

Here is a picture of the Tower of London, drawn in 1753. Do you notice the coach in the foreground? And all those masts and *pennants* beyond the Tower? They belong to ships anchored at Tower Wharf; many ships used to unload their goods here.

In the eighteenth century the Tower of London served many purposes, but it was no longer used as a royal palace as it had once been. The Governor of the Tower lived in what was once the King's House, a fine Tudor building facing the Inner Court of the Tower. Important prisoners were kept in the Tower.

I must tell you one exciting adventure story that took place in the Tower during our eighteenth century.

In 1715 some Scottish nobles led a revolt to try and restore the son of King James II to the throne. James II had fled from Britain in 1688 when the last revolution took place. These nobles thought that James II's son, whom they called James III, had a better right to the throne of England than King George I, a German who could not even speak English. The rebels were defeated and among those captured and brought to London was a Scottish nobleman named Lord Nithsdale. He was tried and condemned to death, but his wife, who was a brave and devoted lady, was determined to rescue him, although he was imprisoned in the Tower of London.

Lord Nithsdale was held in a room in the Lieutenant's Lodgings. Outside his window was a forty-foot drop to the path below and there was always a guard outside his door, so it looked as though escape was impossible. But on February 23, 1716, Lady Nithsdale, accompanied by two ladies, went to say farewell to her husband. While she was with him, first one lady came in, said goodbye to his lordship and left, and then the other lady came to do the same. Both left behind some article of clothing. Lord Nithsdale quickly put on these women's clothes as well as a wig and with a hood drawn over his face he left the room on his wife's arm, pretending to be weeping into a large handkerchief. The guards thought it was one of Lady Nithsdale's companions and allowed them to pass.

Outside, Lady Nithsdale saw her husband into a coach and then returned to the room and carried on an imaginary conversation as though he was still in his prison cell. Later she left and told the guard her husband was at his prayers and did not wish to be disturbed—she hoped this way that more time would be gained for the escape. The coach had driven safely away and Lady Nithsdale followed it. Then she managed to get her husband engaged as a servant to the Venetian Ambassador, who was about to leave London. So Lord Nithsdale escaped from England. His wife rejoined him in Rome and they lived there happily until the Earl's death in 1744.

London in a Panic

Lord Nithsdale had been condemned to death for his part in the rebellion of 1715. Thirty years later there was another rebellion, called 'The Forty-Five'.

The son of James III, Prince Charles Edward, was known as Bonnie Prince Charlie to his supporters, and 'the Young Pretender' to his foes. After a great deal of plotting and planning abroad he went to Scotland, where there were many people who supported the Jacobite cause —this was the name given to those who believed James III to be the rightful king and it was taken from the Latin name 'Jacobus', which means James.

The Scottish clans rallied to Prince Charles Edward's standard and at first everything went well. They won several battles and marched south into England.

When the news reached London that the Prince's army had got as far as Derby, everyone in London became very frightened—they imagined a great many wild Highland men descending on London and burning all their houses down and stealing all their goods. The bad news reached London on Friday, December 6, 1745, a day at once called

78

'Black Friday', and there was panic in the City. People hurried to draw their money out of the Bank of England in case they had to leave London at a moment's notice. The Royal Exchange became a barracks for London's *train-bands*, the City's own soldiers, and the night guards were stationed in Bridewell prison. The lawyers of the City formed themselves into a regiment and they said they would act as a bodyguard to the Royal Family if the King took command of the Guards, as he said he would.

The King's second son, the Duke of Cumberland, was, however, sent north at the head of the army. The news soon reached London that the Jacobite army was retreating to Scotland, and London was able to breathe freely again. Everyone felt they had been rather silly to get in such a panic. In April of the next year, 1746, the Prince's army was defeated on Culloden Moor, and though the Prince escaped, there were no more Jacobite risings.

Below you can see the two sides of a medal struck to commemorate the victory at Culloden:

But though there were no more risings, there were still many people who were Jacobites at heart. There are many well-known Jacobite songs. I expect you know one or two of them without ever having realized that they were Jacobite songs. 'Charlie is my darling' is one, and 'Will ye no come back again?' is another, and I'm sure you know the Skye Boat song:

> Speed bonny boat like a bird on the wing,
> 'Onward' the sailors cry.
> Carry the lad that's born to be King,
> Over the sea to Skye.

Did you know this song was written about Bonny Prince Charlie's escape, dressed as a maid, in a little boat that crossed from the mainland of Scotland to the island of Skye?

For a long time after the rising of the '45, Jacobites used to meet at the WHITE COCK tavern in the Strand, and there sing their songs and toast their 'King over the water'. They used to hold their wine-glasses over a bowl of water, drinking the health of 'His Majesty the King', but meaning not King George in London, but James or his son who lived in exile abroad.

HIS MAJESTY THE KING

Dr. Burney came to his new house in St. Martin's Street in the same year as George III came to the throne.

The reign of George III began very well, for the new king was a young man eager to be a good king. Unlike his German father and grandfather, he had grown up in England and loved the country. One of the first things he did as king was to issue a proclamation that he 'gloried in the name of Briton'. He and his young wife, Queen Charlotte, were determined to do their best for the country. As Fanny Burney held the post of second Keeper of the Robes to the Queen at a salary of £200 a year, she can tell us something of the young King and Queen. This is what she wrote in her diary about the royal couple:

> The Queen indeed is a most charming woman—she appears to me full of sense and graciousness. . . . She speaks English almost perfectly well, with great choice . . . of language, though frequently with a foreign accent. Her manners have an easy dignity with a most engaging simplicity.
>
> The King has in private the appearance of a character the most open and sincere. He speaks his opinions without reserve and seems to trust them to his hearers from a belief that they will make no ill use of them.
>
> Their behaviour to each other speaks the most cordial confidence and happiness. The King seems to admire as much as he enjoys her conversation and to *covet* her *participation* in everything he either sees or hears. The Queen appears to feel the most grateful regard for him, and to make it her chief study to raise his *consequence* with others.

Indeed, in their different ways they left me charmed with their behaviour to each other.

You see how much Fanny admires her King and Queen. Here is a little conversation between them which she records in her diary. The King has remarked how time flies

"O, for me," cried the Queen, "I am always quarrelling with time—it is so short to do something and so long to do nothing."

"Time," said the King, "always seems so long when we are young and so short when we begin to grow old."

"But nothing makes me so angry," the Queen said, "as to hear people not know what to do. For me, I never have half time enough for things. But what makes me most angry still is to see people go up to a window and say, 'What a bad day! What shall we do such a day as this?' Now I say 'Why, employ yourselves and then what signifies a bad day?'"

Do you think Queen Charlotte was right?

The King and Queen often stayed at Windsor Palace or Hampton Court Palace. They would drive from one of their palaces to another in a carriage like this one:

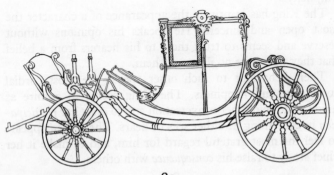

Their main London home was St. James's Palace and below you will see what it looked like in the eighteenth century:

Do you see the building on the left at the end of St. James's Park? That is the home of our present Queen—Buckingham Palace. It was built in 1705 for the Duke of Buckingham and called Buckingham House, but in 1762 George III bought it and it became his family home. Parts of the Palace have been altered since his day, but the gates and the main front shown in this picture look much the same today.

Although Buckingham Palace has become their London home, St. James's Palace remains the official headquarters of the Royal Family. All the Court news is given "from our Palace of St. James's", and the Sovereign is always proclaimed King or Queen from the balcony there.

It is a small palace, and with its mellow red brick walls it has a pleasant homely air. It is used today mainly for receptions, banquets and *investitures*.

GOODBYE LONDON

I hope that during our walks round eighteenth-century London, you have managed to picture in your mind what kind of a place it was, full of life and colour and gaiety. Let us take a last walk down the Strand with its busy shops and watch the people as they hurry about their business. Above our heads the inn signs swing gaily in the morning breeze and there is a delicious smell coming from the coffee-houses.

Men on horseback, carriages and sedan-chairs pass up and down the street and we may see a group of soldiers ride by.

On the way we are jostled by the pedlars and ballad-mongers and by the girls selling fruit and fish and all manner of goods. A beggar asks us for a penny and we will give him a few coppers as we want it to be as nice a day for him as it is for us.

We must hurry on towards London Bridge and cross over the river with its busy water traffic. As we walk we can watch the barges and ferries passing up and down and across the river, and listen to the peal of bells ringing out from the church of St. Mary-le-Bow.

Soon we are back at the George Inn, Southwark, and there are the horses already harnessed to the stage-coach waiting to take us home.

Goodbye, eighteenth-century London, goodbye!

HOW WE CAN FIND 'THEN' IN LONDON NOW

Probably when you visit London—and if you live there—you hurry along looking into the shops, riding on buses or trains, or going to the cinema, so you may not realize that the London of the past is all round you if only you will look for it. For those of you who are in London, here are some suggestions as to how you can set about looking for the past.

Go to your school or public library and find a good book about Old London—there are plenty of these, and one of the best is by Arthur Mee. Look up a street that is well known, such as the Strand, or Fleet Street, or Cheapside, and find out all you can about it. Then go to this street and walk up and down it using your eyes. You will find an old building here, an ancient church there, a narrow alley or a quiet square, that were much the same in the eighteenth century. London is full of surprises, and the busiest street is often the place where we can find many signs of the past.

Remember always to look up at the walls of the houses. There is often a blue plate that tells you that some famous person was born or lived in that house. For instance, in Church Street, Kensington, you can see a blue plate that tells you that the composer, Mendelssohn, lived there for a while. What music did Mendelssohn write? You will find other notices, too, sometimes. For instance, there is a notice in the front of St. Paul's Church, Covent Garden, that David Garrick was baptized there and Dr. Arne worshipped and was buried here. Do you remember reading about the tune you know that was composed by Dr. Arne?

As you walk along, try to picture the street as it was two hundred years ago. You should buy or borrow a small guide-book with a map of London that will help you to explore.

When you walk about London make sure you look in the old bookshops, for often you will find prints of Old London. Some are quite cheap: so perhaps you can buy one and frame it yourself for your bedroom. Even if you do not live in London you may find some of these prints in the second-hand bookshops—for every town has these, particularly old cathedral or market towns. So walk about with your eyes open and see what you can find.

In your public library you can find guide-books about London, and books of pictures—both photographs and old prints. Ask your librarian to help you find some books about London, and about the famous people you have met in this book.

Here are some places which you must try to visit:

1. Southwark Cathedral, and the George Inn nearby.

2. St. Martin-in-the-Fields in Trafalgar Square. Don't forget to go down into the crypt, where you will see a model of the church made by the architect, James Gibbs, when he began the work of rebuilding the old church in 1721.

3. Westminster Abbey. Many famous men have been buried here. Can you find the tombs of Dr. Johnson, David Garrick, and John Gay? Make a list of all the other great men who were alive in 1760 to whom tombstones and tablets have been erected in the Abbey.

4. St. Paul's Cathedral. Many other famous Englishmen were buried here. Can you find the tomb of Sir Joshua Reynolds and the monument to him? What did Fanny Burney write in her diary about Sir Joshua?

5. Whitehall. Notice that Horse Guards Parade and the Clock Tower remain exactly as they look in the picture on page 14. On the opposite side of the road you can see the old Banqueting Hall, now a museum.

6. The Tower of London. This is packed full of exciting things to see. When you look at the King's House remember the story of Lord Nithsdale and think how clever his wife was to help him escape from such a fortress.

7. Greenwich Palace. This is now the Maritime Museum and full of interesting things concerning the sea. It was once a palace. Try to go there by river steamer and remember you are travelling the same way that the kings and queens took by royal barge.

8. Hammersmith Mall, Cheyne Row in Chelsea, and Church Row in Hampstead will all show you how charmingly the eighteenth-century architects could design streets.

9. Ken Wood House, Hampstead. This is a wonderful example of Robert Adam's work and will show you the sort of house the wealthy people lived in during the time we have been learning about in this book.

MUSEUMS

1. Geffrye Museum. This is in the City near Liverpool Street station. Here you can particularly see the sort of furniture that people used about 1760. In what ways is it different from the furniture in our homes today?

2. London Museum. You can have a pleasant walk through Kensington Gardens to visit this fascinating museum which tells you the story of London from the very earliest times to the present. You can see models of old London and an eighteenth-century shop-front as well as many clothes of the period.

3. The Victoria and Albert Museum. This is in South Kensington, and here you will find out all about home life through the centuries in England—you can see clothes and furniture, pictures and ornaments, and even carriages and sedan chairs. Can you find the desk that Oliver Goldsmith used?

4. Hogarth Museum. This is a little way out of central London, in Chiswick, but it is well worth a visit because Hogarth once lived in the house and it is full of his possessions and pictures. We owe much of our knowledge of the eighteenth century to his painting.

THINGS TO MAKE AND DO

EARLY MORNING IN LONDON

1. Compare the sounds you hear with eighteenth-century sounds. Which is the noisier century, do you think?

2. Do you hear any street-cries today? Make a list of as many as you can. (This can include the shouts of barrow-boys.)

3. Make a small cardboard measuring-wheel (see page 5) showing inches, and measure your desk or table with it.

A WALK ROUND THE TOWN

1. Could you draw or paint either the busy scene in the yard of the George Inn or London Bridge as it was in the eighteenth century?

2. See if you can make up a ballad about some special happening in your district, or in your family life—perhaps a local fair or a family birthday.

3. You have learned how people went from place to place in London two hundred years ago. Make a list of the various ways of travel then, and another of the means of transport today.

4. See if you can draw and paint a sign to hang outside a shop. It must show clearly what the shop sells.

FANNY BURNEY AND HER FAMILY

1. Compare the furniture the Burneys used with your own and see how styles have changed.

2. If you have a famous house open to the public in your district, go and see it. Is there a four-poster bed there?

3. Girls—see if you can make a dress for your doll like the one belonging to the lady on page 19.

4. Write down the meals you had yesterday and compare them with the meals on pages 27 and 64.

5. Write an account of an eighteenth-century dinner party as if you had been there.

1. Boys: make up a pattern for a sampler and see if the girls in your class can sew it.

2. Make a list of all the different subjects you are taught and see how many more things you learn about than the children of two hundred years ago.

GOING TO CHURCH

1. Visit your own parish church and see if you can find any memorials on the walls dating from the eighteenth century.

2. Ask the verger to tell you the history of the church and write it down when you get home.

FAMOUS VISITORS IN ST. MARTIN'S STREET

1. Choose one of the visitors to the Burneys' household and make your own book about him—find out everything you can from encyclopedias and public libraries until you have written down the story of his life.

2. If you are ever in London, visit Dr. Johnson's house in Gough Square, which is on the North side of Fleet Street. This is the only house standing today which we are certain he lived in, and it was here that he wrote his famous dictionary.

HOW THE RICH PEOPLE ENJOY THEMSELVES

1. See if you can draw a sedan chair with the link boys running ahead with their lighted torches.

2. Could you write and act a play about a highwayman holding up a coach?

3. Look through your *Radio Times* and see if you can find out when some of Handel's music is being played and listen to it. You will certainly be able to hear some of 'Messiah' at Christmas either on the radio or perhaps at your local church or concert hall.

4. Write an imaginary account of a visit to one of the Pleasure Gardens, such as Ranelagh or Vauxhall.

LIFE IN THE HOUSE OF ROBERT GIBBON, DRAPER

1. Could you draw a shop-bill for a draper's or a bookshop or perhaps a saddler's?

2. See if you can find out what trades in your town employ apprentices and on what conditions. Compare these with the life of Tom or Ralph.

3. See how many items on the list of expenses on page 63 you can compare with today's prices, and see what costs more and what is cheaper.

4. Write your own account of a day in the life of an apprentice two hundred years ago.

WHAT HAPPENED WHEN YOU WERE ILL

1. Draw a picture or write a story about a beggar leaving a baby at the Foundling Hospital.

2. Find out when your local hospital was built and who were its most important benefactors.

THE LORD MAYOR OF LONDON

1. Find out what you can about the duties of the Mayor of your own town, or the Lord Mayor if you live in London.

2. See if you can draw a picture of the Tower.

3 Write and act the story of Lord Nithsdale's famous escape.

HIS MAJESTY THE KING

1. If you live in London, try to visit the National Portrait Gallery and see the pictures of our eighteenth-century kings and queens.

2. On page 82 the Queen says you should "employ yourselves" on a wet day. If you were an eighteenth-century boy or girl, what would you do?

GLOSSARY

alderman : chief officer of a *ward*; elected for life.

apothecary : old name for a chemist.

apprentice : boy learning a trade.

backgammon: game like draughts but played with dice.

ballad : simple song, often telling a well known story.

banquet : feast or rich entertainment.

beadle : man who kept order before there were policemen.

biography : story of a man's life.

canopy : covering hung on posts over a bed.

catechism : book of religious instruction by means of question and answer learnt by heart.

chaise : light low carriage pulled by ponies.

chandelier : frame hanging from ceiling with branches for candles.

chutney : sweet pickle.

cockpit : place where cock-fighting took place.

comedian : man who acts comic parts in plays.

common councilmen: men elected to govern the City of London.

consequence: importance.

cordials : refreshing drinks.

coroner : man who enquires into the cause of sudden deaths.

countenance : face.

covet : to want eagerly.

damask : silk with patterns on it that used to come from Damascus.

dispensary : place where medicine can be obtained.

foppery : vanity in dress or manners.

foundlings: babies left by parents for others to find and look after.

freeman: man with right to trade in a city and vote in its elections.

fuller's earth : kind of clay used for cleaning cloth.

galleries : raised places for sitting or walking inside or outside a building.

grotto : imitation cave.

guild : society of craftsmen of a particular trade.

harpsichord : early form of piano.

holland : kind of fine linen material, first made in Holland.

indentures : legal documents prepared and signed by the guardian and by the employer of an *apprentice.*

indigo : blue powder used as a dye.

investiture : ceremony at which medals and titles are received.

journeyman : craftsman working for a master and earning a wage.

kennel : channel or gutter in a street.

liveryman : member of a guild entitled to wear its uniform or livery.

mitre : tall cap worn by bishops.

ostler : man who attends to horses at an inn.

participate : share in.

pedlar : man who travelled about on foot, selling small articles.

pennants : small flags often used for sending signals from ships.

periwig : small wig.

phaeton : light four-wheeled open carriage usually drawn by a pair of horses.

physician : doctor.

playwright : man who writes plays.

prescribe : to write directions for the preparation of medicine.

quadrille : old-fashioned dance.

sampler : piece of material on which different sorts of embroidery stitches are practised.

sedan-chair : box-like carriage carried on poles by two men.

sewer : covered drain.

sheriff : man in charge of keeping law and order in a county.

sonorous : deep toned.

squire : most important land-owner in a village.

surgeon : man who performs operations.

taffeta : thin glossy silk fabric.

tavern : old name for an inn or 'public house'.

tenant : man who rents his land, house or shop from a landlord.

tincture : small amount.

topographer : man who makes maps.

train-band : group of citizens trained to use weapons.

ward : small areas into which a borough or city is divided.

watermen : men who ferried people and goods up and down the river.